D1784161

Practice Tests for Key Stage 2

English

Photocopymasters

John Aldridge

Keith Gaines

Oxford University Press

Acknowledgements
The poems, 'Books' by John Kitching and
'The Dragon of Death' by Jack Prelutsky, are
taken from *A Fifth Poetry Book*, compiled by
John Foster and published by Oxford
University Press, 1985. 'The Dragon of Death'
was also published in *Nightmares and other
poems to trouble your sleep*, by Jack Prelutsky,
published by A & C Black.

The text for 'Gold' and 'Medals' has been
adapted from the *Oxford Children's
Encyclopedia* published by Oxford University
Press, 1991.

Many thanks to the editorial team at
Aldridge Press: Charlotte Rolfe, Sarah
Henderson, Felix Muriithi, Mark Wightwick,
Jocelyne and David.

Oxford University Press, Walton Street, Oxford
OX2 6DP

Oxford New York
Athens Auckland Bangkok Bombay
Calcutta Cape Town Dar es Salaam Delhi
Florence Hong Kong Istanbul Karachi
Kuala Lumpur Madras Madrid Melbourne
Mexico City Nairobi Paris Singapore
Taipei Tokyo Toronto

and associated companies in
Berlin Ibadan

Oxford is a trade mark of Oxford University Press

© John Aldridge and Keith Gaines 1996
First published 1996
Reprinted as photocopymasters 1996

ISBN 0 19 838197 2

Designed by Geoffrey Wadsley
Illustrations by Julia Osorno
The Keith Gaines Archive
Packaged by Aldridge Press

Printed in Great Britain

Individual pages of this book may be reproduced by
individual teachers for class use within the
purchaser's institution. The material remains
copyright under the Copyright, Designs and Patents
Act, 1988, or in the case of reprographic reproduction
in accordance with the terms of licences issued by
the Copyright Licensing Agency. No part of this
publication may be reproduced for other purposes
without prior permission of Oxford University Press.
Enquiries concerning reproduction outside those
terms and in other countries should be sent to the
Rights Department, Oxford University Press, at the
address above.

• Contents •

Using these tests

Who are these tests for?

- These photocopiable tests have been designed for pupils aged 10-11, in their final year of primary school. They can also be used with pupils in their penultimate year of primary school.

- The questions in the tests cover Levels 2 to 6 of the National Curriculum with particular emphasis on Levels 3, 4 and 5, and can give useful practice for the national Key Stage 2 tests.

- The English skills which are assessed in the tests are:

  1. Reading fiction
  2. Reading non-fiction
  3. Reading poetry
  4. Writing fiction (stories) and non-fiction (letters)
  5. Spelling
  6. Handwriting

  The content of the tests and the style of the questions matches what is covered in the national tests.

How can practice tests help your pupils?

- The Key Stage 2 tests for English, covering Levels 3 to 6 of the National Curriculum, are intended to be an external measurement of pupils' attainment in the National Curriculum. This measurement is then reported to parents, together with the Teacher's Assessment.

- These practice tests can provide valuable opportunities for sharing with children an analysis and a discussion of their work. In the various tasks, pupils can be shown how their performance met – or did not meet – the criteria being used to assess performance. The intention of these practice tests is to help pupils to become more aware of how they can show their full potential in the Key Stage 2 tests.

- Group tests can be used to give a class experience of test conditions and test formats, so that the experience of formal Key Stage 2 tests is not totally alien. For example, some children have underperformed by stopping at the first question they could not answer and failing to complete the whole test. Others have lost marks by not checking back over their answers. Some pupils were simply unfamiliar with a multiple choice format.

- All pencil and paper tests such as these and the Key Stage 2 tests have limitations. AT1 – Speaking and listening – is not assessed, nor do the test scores and levels achieved take account of teacher assessment.

Using the tests

There are 6 tests in this photocopymaster pack. Five of the tests are divided into sub-tests in order to give pupils an opportunity to practise the full range of question types included in the national tests. Where there are two or three sub-tests (eg 1a and 1b), Test a has been constructed so that it is generally easier to read and to answer than test b. It is recommended that each sub-test is given on a separate occasion, or that at least a short break takes place between different tests.

Test 1 comprises two tests which are about reading fiction and which examine your pupils' ability to read and to understand what they are reading. There are two sub-tests:
Test 1a Fiction: Midas – the King with the Golden Touch, and
Test 1b Fiction: The Interest on Ten Shillings

Test 2 comprises two tests which are about reading non-fiction. Like Test 1, they examine your pupils' ability to read the words and to understand the content. There are two sub-tests:
Test 2a Non-fiction: Gold!
Test 2b Non-fiction: Precious Objects – Jewellery, Charms and Medals

Test 3 contains two tests which are about reading and understanding poetry. Again there are two sub-tests:
Test 3a Poetry: The Dragon of Death
Test 3b Poetry: Golden Glories

Test 4 contains two activities which give your pupils an opportunity to display their skills in composing written English. There are two parts :
Test 4a Story writing: in which the children write a fictional story.
Test 4b Letter writing: which examines factual and functional writing.

Test 5, the Spelling tests, is in three parts of increasing difficulty:
Test 5a Spelling
Test 5b Spelling
Test 5c Spelling

Test 6 enables you to assess your pupils' handwriting, when they are concentrating only on handwriting and not the other skills involved in written English.

- The length of each test will vary, dependent on what is being assessed and your pupils' own abilities in reading, writing and thinking. Most tests should take pupils between 15 and 40 minutes to complete.

- Encourage them to do as much as possible but allow them to stop when they want to – remember that these are only practice tests!

Materials needed

- pen or pencil, paper (lined or unlined – whichever your pupils are used to) for Tests 4a and 4b, the Writing Tests. A rubber may be used for corrections, although no marks are deducted for crossings-out.

Instructions to pupils

- You can ask pupils to write their names and the start and finish times on the test. Encourage your pupils to work swiftly but carefully.

- Have a quick look through each test before your pupils begin and use your common sense in deciding how much advice and instruction to give. Wherever instructions are printed on the test pages, you may read these to your pupils if you think this would be appropriate and helpful.

- As in the Key Stage 2 tests, you should not say anything which will give them the answer, but you can give pupils lots of encouragement and reassurance.

- **The Reading Tests:** Before your pupils begin a Reading Test, you may find it helpful to say something along these lines:

  'Read the whole passage (or poem) very carefully. Look at the pictures because they should help you. After the passage, there are some questions which have to be answered. The questions are in the tinted boxes and the pencil will show where to write your answer. Sometimes there are four answers given underneath the question. You have to draw a line under the right answer. Sometimes there are boxes for you to put a tick or a cross in. Sometimes you have to write an answer in words or sentences. If you are not sure how to answer a question, just ask me.'

- You might like to add:–
  'Some of the questions are quite difficult and you may not be able to do these. Try all the questions but if you can't do one don't worry, just move on to the next question. At the end of the test go back and have another go at any you found difficult the first time.'

- **The Writing Tests:** Basic instructions are given on the pupils' pages (44 to 47). For this test pupils will need paper to write on (lined or unlined – whichever they are used to). Tell your pupils that they should concentrate on writing a good story or letter – spelling and handwriting are not assessed at all in this activity. Try to avoid discussing pupils' writing while the test is being done. This could be the longest test for some children.

- **The Spelling Tests:** Full instructions are given on pages 61 and 62.

- **The Handwriting Test:** Instructions are given on the test (page 51).

Marking the tests

A full guide to marking is given on pages 52 to 63. For some questions, especially those where pupils have to write their own sentences as an answer, there could be a very wide variety of correct and incorrect answers. Guidance is given, but you will probably find several places where you simply have to use your own judgement as to whether the answer merits 1, 2 or 3 marks.

Finding the English level

At the end of the answers for each test there is a guide to how your pupils have done in terms of National Curriculum Levels. An overall National Curriculum level for English can be found using the chart on page 64.

Midas
the King with the Golden Touch

Long, long ago, King Midas ruled over the country of Phrygia. He was a wise and just king and Dionysus, the Greek god of the countryside, decided to reward Midas with a gift.

'I love gold,' said Midas. 'Grant me the power to change everything I touch into gold.'

'Are you sure?' asked Dionysus, in a deep booming voice.

'Of course I'm sure,' cried Midas. 'I'll live in a golden house. I'll sit in a golden chair. I'll sleep in a golden bed. I'll be the richest man in the world.'

'How will you walk, wearing heavy stiff golden clothes?' asked the god.

'Oh, I never thought of that,' said Midas. 'All right. Grant me the power to change everything I touch into gold, except my clothes.'

'So be it,' said the god. 'Your wish is granted, but it may bring you great sorrow. Remember, everything you touch will be turned to gold.'

'Gold! Gold!' Midas shouted to his wife. 'Everything in my palace will be gold.'

'You've gone mad,' said the Queen. 'Go and have a lie down until you feel better.'

'Watch this!' cried Midas.

He sat on his wooden throne. As his hands touched it, the throne became solid gold.

'That's clever,' said the Queen. 'How did you do that? Does it work on anything?'

Just then, the King's dog ran up to Midas.

© O.U.P. 1996

'Good boy!' said the King, forgetfully patting him on the head.

'Oh dear,' said Midas, as the dog turned into a golden statue. 'What a shame!'

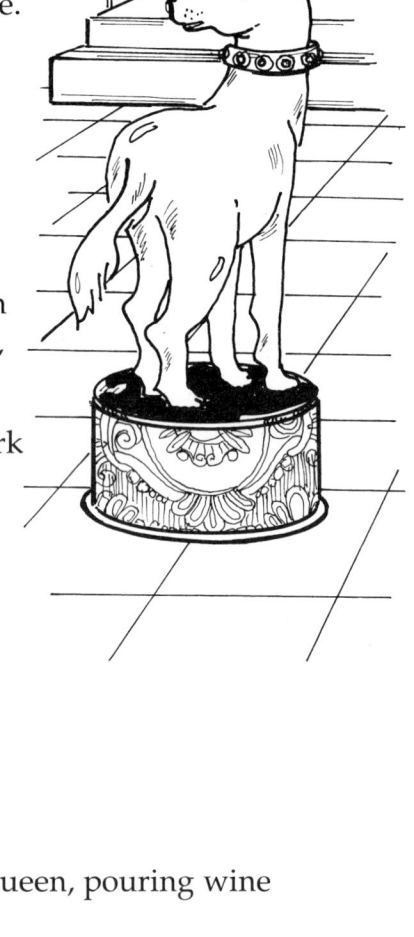

'Never mind,' said the Queen. 'I'm sure a golden dog will look very nice in the hallway.'

'I'm hungry!' exclaimed Midas. 'It must be all this gold-making. What's for dinner?'

'We've got a nice salad,' said the Queen, 'with some chicken left over from yesterday. And since you are now so wealthy, I'll open a bottle of the best wine to celebrate.'

His dinner was set before him and Midas stuck a golden fork into a piece of chicken.

The fork bent. He tried his knife, but that bent as well.

'It's because you've made them into gold,' said the Queen. 'Pure gold is very soft.'

'I'll use my fingers,' said Midas, picking up a piece of meat.

'This chicken's gone hard!'

He looked at the meat. It was gold.

'Try a cup of wine,' said the Queen, pouring wine into a wooden cup.

By the time the cup reached the King's mouth it had become a gold wine cup. He sniffed the wine. 'Ahh! You can tell just by the smell that this is an excellent vintage.'

Midas sipped the wine.

© O.U.P. 1996

'Mmm! That's really … HORRIBLE!' Midas spat out the wine. A little shower of gold drops, as delicate as the finest jewellery, clattered onto the table.

'This is serious,' said Midas. 'I can't eat or drink.'

Just then his little daughter ran in.

'Hello, Daddy,' cried the Princess. 'Let me give you a kiss.'

She flung her arms around her father's neck.

'Don't touch me!' yelled the king. But it was too late. He watched in horror as his beloved child turned into a gold statue.

'Oh great Dionysus,' implored Midas. 'Please rid me of this deadly curse.'

'There is a way,' said the god gently. 'Go and bathe in the river Pactolus. Its waters will wash away the power of the golden touch. Bring back some of the river water and sprinkle it over those things you turned into gold.'

Midas went to the river and plunged in. The water around him turned yellow, then cleared as tiny particles of gold sank down to the river bottom. When Midas sprinkled the river water over his daughter, the gold colour drained away from her body as she became flesh and blood again.

'Now for the dog,' said Midas.

'Are you sure?' asked the Queen. 'I quite like the golden dog in the hallway. It's very useful for hanging coats on.'

'Yes,' said Midas. 'I am sure. I never want to see gold again anywhere in my kingdom!'

But to this very day, tiny bits of gold can still be found in the mud of the river Pactolus, in the land of Phrygia.

© O.U.P. 1996

• Test 1a Reading fiction •

Time started   :

Time finished   :

Midas – the King with the Golden Touch

The questions on the next four pages are all about the story *Midas – the King with the Golden Touch*. When you are thinking of the answers, you can look back at the story any time you want.

Draw a line under the correct answer when required.

1   Midas was king of

Lydia	Phrygia	Dionysus	Greece

☐

2   Dionysus warned that the golden touch would bring Midas

gold	riches	chickens	sorrow

☐

3   When Midas came in shouting 'Gold! Gold!', the queen thought he was

angry	ill	crazy	joking

☐

4   Midas turned his dog into gold because

he wanted a golden dog	the Queen wanted to hang coats on the dog
Midas forgot he had the golden touch	it was a golden retriever

☐

© O.U.P. 1996

PAGE TOTAL

5 The Princess turned to gold because

she touched her
father's neck

Midas wanted a golden
statue of her

Midas kissed her

she touched the
golden dog

☐

6 How did Midas lose the golden touch?

he drank river water

he turned a river into gold

he bathed in a river

it wore off

☐

7 Who came back to life again?

just the dog

the Princess and the dog

just the Princess

the dog and the Queen

☐

8 How much gold did Midas want at the beginning of the story?

none at all   just a little   lots   just a golden dog   ☐

9 How much gold did Midas want at the end of the story?

none at all   just a little   lots   just a golden dog   ☐

10 Where do you think this story was first told?

ancient Greece   ancient Rome   ancient Britain   ☐

© O.U.P. 1996

PAGE TOTAL

11 Put a tick (✓) by all the things in the story which King Midas turned into gold. Put a cross (✗) in the box by anything which King Midas did not turn into gold in this story.

his throne	☐	his table	☐	his cat	☐
his horse	☐	his hair	☐	his bed	☐
his daughter	☐	his dinner	☐	his knife	☐
his wife	☐	his clothes	☐	his jewellery	☐
his dog	☐	his wine cup	☐	his wine	☐

12 Why do you think Midas described the golden touch as a 'deadly curse'?

✎ --

----

13 Which of these words best describes what Midas felt about gold at the beginning of the story?

indifference   boredom   interest   greed

14 What kind of person do you think the Queen was?

✎ --

----

15 Which word in the first paragraph of the story means 'clever' and 'sensible'?

✎ --

16 Which **two** words describe the voice of Dionysus?

✎ **(a)** ----------------------------   **(b)** ----------------------------

© O.U.P. 1996

PAGE TOTAL

17 Look at the second paragraph on page 9. Why do you think Midas said 'This is serious'?

✎ ---

□
□

----

18 Did you like this story?

Yes □   No □

Why? ✎ ---

□
□

----

19 Would you like to be given the golden touch?

Yes □   No □

Explain the reasons for your answer.

✎ ---

□
□

----

20 Today people sometimes describe a person working in business or entertainment as 'having the golden touch'. What do you think they mean by this?

✎ ---

□
□

© O.U.P. 1996

PAGE TOTAL

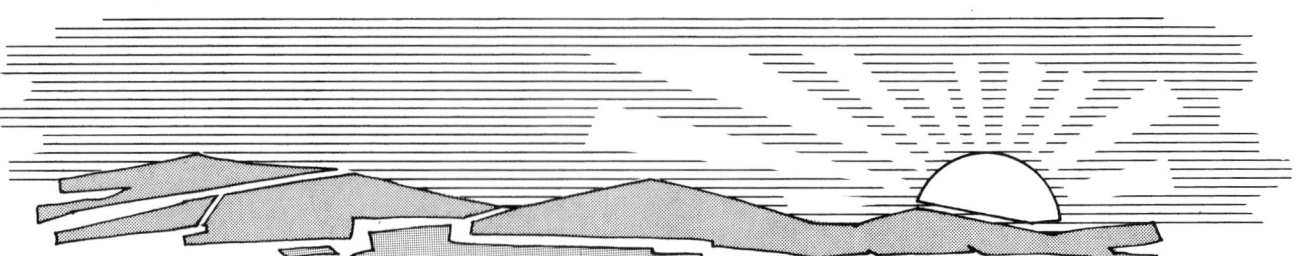

The Interest on Ten Shillings

A hundred years ago Henry Rider Haggard's books were very popular. Some, like 'King Solomon's Mines' and 'She', are still in book shops today. Many of his stories were set in Africa and featured Allan Quartermain, the elephant-hunter. In this extract, old 'Hunter' Quartermain remembers the time when he lost ten shillings (50 pence) but found a fortune, and this is what he said:

Ah! yes, I once went gold-mining at Pilgrim's Rest in South Africa. It was in a stony valley, with mountains all around. Many's the time I threw down my pick and shovel in disgust, clambered out of my claim, and walked a couple of miles to the top of some hill. Lying in the grass, far away from the cursing of the miners and the voices of the Basotho workers as they toiled in the sun, I would look out over the smiling valleys and the great mountains touched with gold – real gold of the sunset.

© O.U.P. 1996

I bought my mine for five hundred pounds, which I thought cheap. The previous owner had made a fortune from it, but I found out later he had got no gold out of it in the past six months. I worked with my son Harry and half a dozen African miners. And we worked, my word, we did work – early and late we went at it – but never a bit of gold did we see; not even a nugget large enough to make a pin. For three months this went on, till I had spent nearly all our money in wages and food.

At last the crisis came. One Saturday night I had paid the men, and bought their food. Harry and I sat on the edge of the great hole we had dug in the hill-side. I pulled out my purse and emptied its contents into my hand. There was a gold half-sovereign, and a few small coins.

'This is all our worldly wealth,' I said; 'that hole has swallowed the rest!'

'Well, father,' said Harry, 'we'll just have to work for other people.'

'Be quiet, boy!' I said, raising my hand as though to hit him. The half-sovereign slipped out of my hand into the gulf below.

'That's what comes of getting angry!' said Harry.

© O.U.P. 1996

We scrambled down to hunt for the coin, but a half-sovereign is hard to see by moonlight and there was loose soil about, for the Africans had been working at this very spot a couple of hours before. I took a pick and raked away with it, but all in vain. At last in sheer annoyance I struck the sharp end of the pickaxe down into the hard soil. To my astonishment it sank right in.

'Why, Harry,' I said, 'this ground has been disturbed!'

'I don't think so, father,' he answered; 'but we will soon see,' and he began to shovel out the soil with his hands. 'It's only some stones,' said Harry, 'the pick has gone down between them.' He pulled out a stone.

'I say, Dad,' he said, almost in a whisper, 'it's precious heavy.' He passed me a brownish lump about the size of an apple. It was very heavy. Curious thrills of excitement began to pass through me. Resting the brown stone on my knee, I scratched at it with my knife. Great heavens, it was soft! Another second and the secret was out. We had found a nugget of pure gold, weighing four pounds or more!

© O.U.P. 1996

Trembling with excitement, we dug with our hands and uncovered a regular nest of nuggets, from the size of a hazel-nut to that of a hen's egg. It turned out that our nuggets were worth twelve hundred and fifty pounds. That's all we ever found and I sold the mine soon after, but I took out of that hole four hundred and fifty pounds more than I put into it – a pretty good interest on my lost ten shillings!

Adapted from 'A tale of three lions' in 'Allan's Wife And Other Tales' by H. Rider Haggard, published by Spencer Blackett, London, 1889.

© O.U.P. 1996

The Interest on Ten Shillings

The questions on the next four pages are all about the story *The Interest on Ten Shillings.* When you are thinking of the answers, you can look back at the story any time you want to.

Draw a line under the correct answer when required.

1 Men worked at the gold mine with

spades   forks   drills   picks and shovels   ☐

2 When Allan bought the mine, he thought the price he had paid for it was

too much   small   fair   a fortune   ☐

3 After working on the mine for three months, Allan thought the mine was

valuable   easy work   too big   a waste of money   ☐

4 When Allan emptied his purse and looked at his money, he had

enough for a month   lots of gold

less than one pound   a fortune   ☐

5 When Allan couldn't find the missing coin he was

annoyed   vain   pleased   tired   ☐

6 How big was the biggest nugget of gold?

like an apple   like a hazel-nut

like a hen's egg   like a pin   ☐

© O.U.P. 1996

7 How much was half a sovereign?

ten shillings (50p)   a shilling (5p)

Over four hundred pounds   10p   ☐

8 What did Harry think was odd when he picked up the stone?

It was dirty.   It was heavy.

It was gold.   It was precious.   ☐

9 How much was Allan's gold worth?

£4   £450   £500   £1250   ☐

10 Which book is the story taken from?

The Interest on Ten Shillings   A Tale of Three Lions

Allan's Wife and Other Tales   King Solomon's Mines   ☐

11 Here are some of the things that happened in the story. Find the event that happened first in the story and write a number 1 in the box next to it. Then find what happened next and write a 2 in the box. Number all the other events in the order that they happened.

Allan and Harry went to look for the lost coin.   ☐

Allan found the stone was gold.   ☐

Allan sold the gold mine.   ☐

Harry pulled out a stone.   ☐

Allan bought a gold mine.   ☐   ☐

Allan dropped a half-sovereign into the mine.   ☐   ☐

© O.U.P. 1996

12 Why do you think Allan believed the gold mine was worth buying?

✎ --

☐

13 The story tells us that Allan dug for gold and that he looked at the mountains and valleys. Which activity do you think he liked doing most?

Digging for gold.   Looking at the mountains and valleys.

☐

What is there in the story which helps you to decide which activity he liked best?

✎ --

☐
☐

14 What kind of person do you think Allan Quartermain was?

✎ --

☐
☐
☐

15 Which word on the second page of the story means 'a large amount of money'?

✎ --

☐

16 Find **four** words in the story which tell you about Allan's feelings at various times.

✎ **(a)** ----------------------- **(c)** -----------------------

(b) ----------------------- **(d)** -----------------------

☐
☐

© O.U.P. 1996

17 The writer uses the sentence 'At last the crisis came.' to introduce the part of the story that takes place on Saturday night. Why do you think he chose to use the word 'crisis'?

✎ ---

☐

18 Did you like this story?

Yes ☐   No ☐

Why?   ✎ --

☐
☐
☐

19 Why do you think the title of this story is 'The Interest on Ten Shillings'?

✎ ---

☐
☐
☐

20 Would you like to dig for gold like Allan Quartermain?

Yes ☐   No ☐

Explain the reasons for your answer.

✎ ---

☐

© O.U.P. 1996

PAGE TOTAL

Gold!

Read about gold through the ages in our feature article on the next four pages, then try to answer the questions about Gold!

Gold

The beauty and rarity of gold, and the fact that it does not rust or tarnish, have made it highly valued throughout history. Pure gold is soft. It is generally hardened by alloying (mixing) it with copper or silver. The gold content of these alloys is measured in carats. Pure gold is said to be 24 carats, whereas an alloy of equal parts of gold and, say, silver is said to be 12-carat gold. Eighteen carat gold is 18/24 pure gold; that is, 75 per cent pure gold.

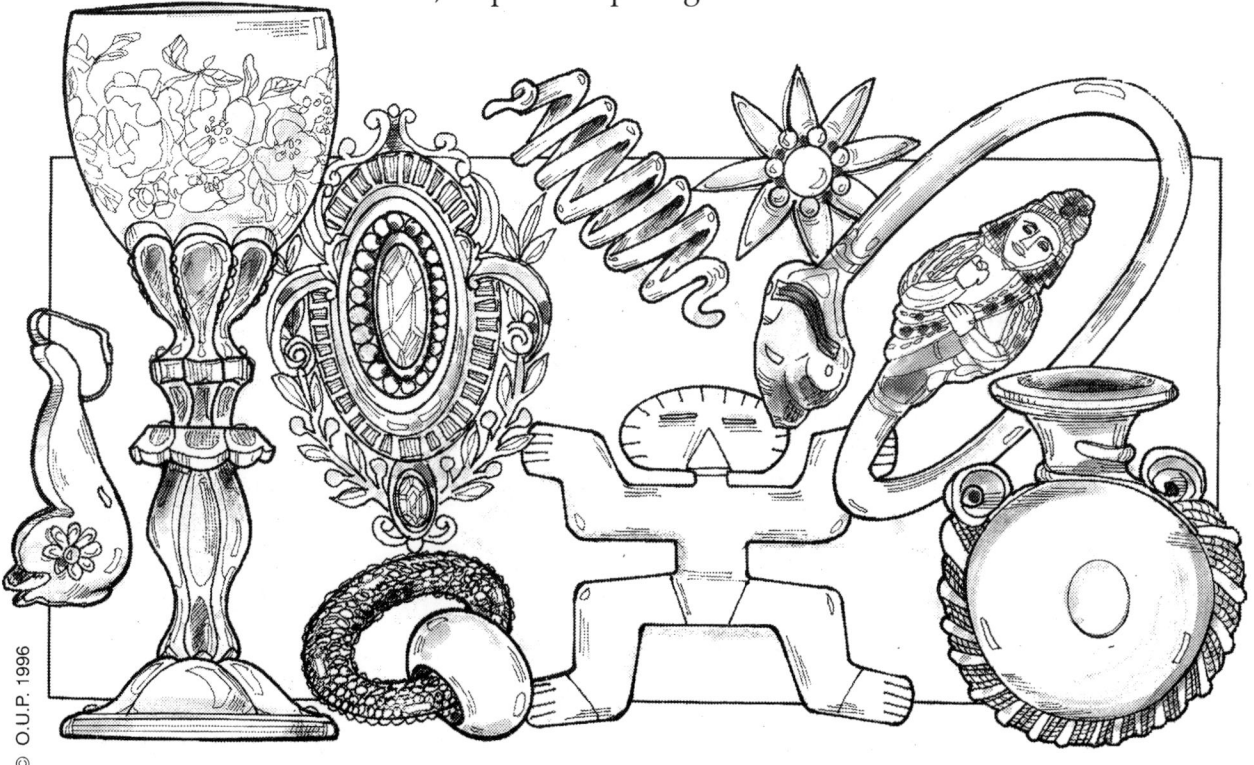

© O.U.P. 1996

Mining and panning for gold

Gold is found as a pure metal. It occurs either in the form of grains in sand and gravel, or as veins in rock. Very occasionally, much larger pieces are found on the surface.

Nowadays, most gold is obtained from mines. The rock is blasted out with explosives and then crushed by heavy machinery. The powdered rock is then treated with chemicals to extract the gold.

Grains of gold are found in the beds of some rivers or streams. This gold can be collected with a shallow metal pan in which the sand and water are carefully swirled around. The sand is washed over the edge, while the gold, which is much heavier, sinks to the bottom.

There is plenty of gold in the sea, but vast amounts of sea water would have to be treated to obtain even a little gold. So far, no one has found a way of doing this cheaply.

© O.U.P. 1996

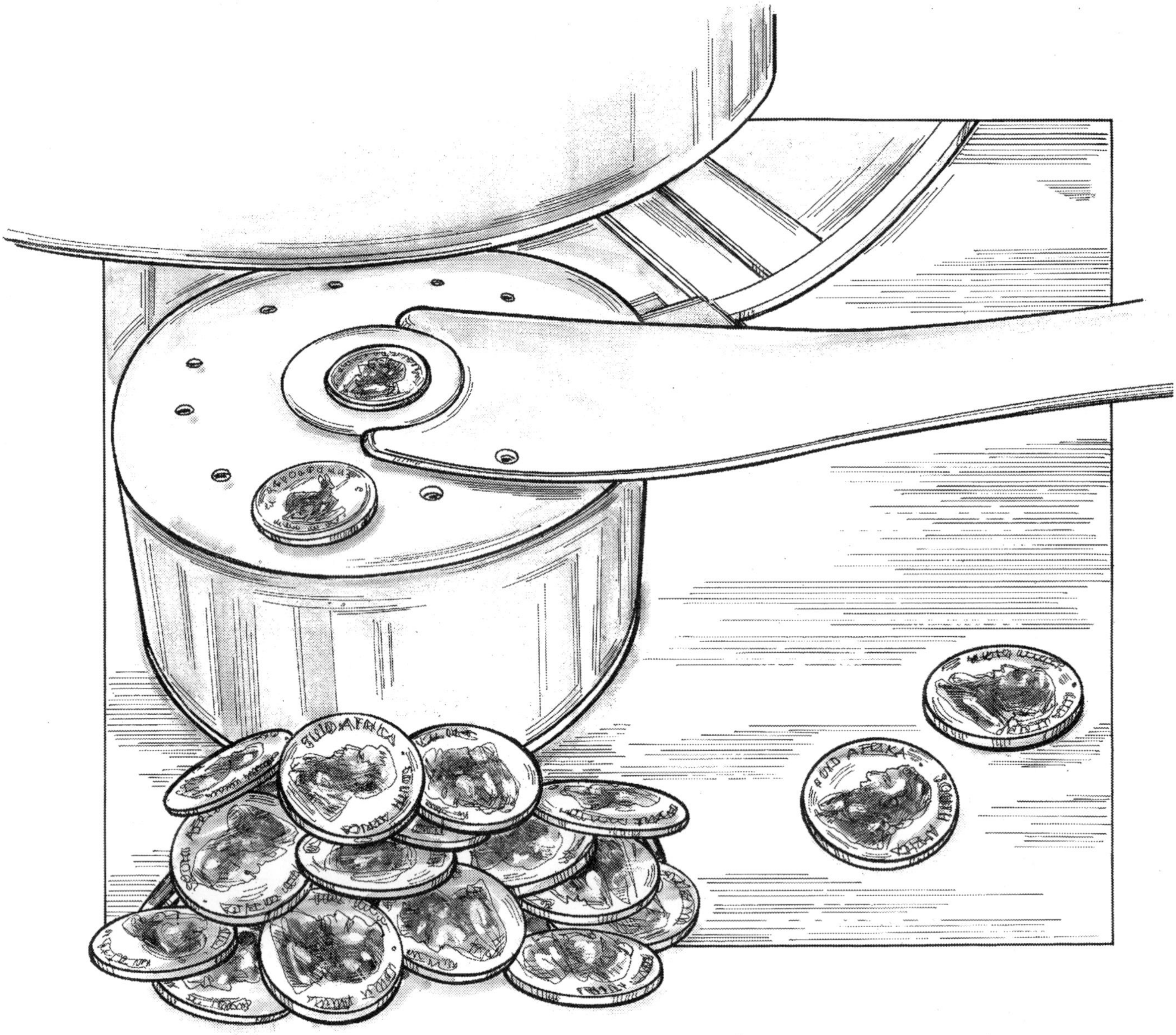

The uses of gold

Gold was first used for coins in about 600 BC by King Croesus of Lydia. Nowadays, countries keep their gold in bank vaults and print paper money instead. Nevertheless, some gold coins are still made for investment, including the British sovereigns and the South African krugerrands.

Gold can easily be hammered into very thin sheets. These sheets are known as gold leaf. Gold leaf is used for gold lettering and for gilding book edges and picture frames. Dentists use gold for filling and capping teeth, while gold, or alloys of gold, is used for making electrical contacts for the electronics industry. The windscreens of jet aircraft are covered with a thin film of gold to cut down glare and to prevent them from icing over.

© O.U.P. 1996

The Star

SOAP BOX

<u>TV1:</u>
5.00: SANTA BARBARA: Keith tells Gina the truth about his feelings on marriage.
5.30: THE YOUNG AND THE RESTLESS

<u>CCV:</u>
4.400: DAYS OF OUR LIVES: Shawn decides to give a bachelor party. And Jack helps Jennifer prepare for Carly's shower.
5.30: THE BOLD AND THE BEAUTIFUL

<u>M-NET:</u>
5.30: LOVING: Cooper turns violent and Trucker tells Stacey he will never forgive Trisha.
6.00:EGOLI: Jane and Arno are uncomfortable about the events of last night.

© O.U.P. 1996

Gold fever!

About 100 tonnes of gold-bearing rock have to be mined to produce just one kilogram of gold!

Gold mining is not easy, but whenever gold has been discovered, people have been drawn by the lure of gold.

In 1851 gold was discovered near Melbourne in Australia. Two years later there were 60,000 gold miners working there.

In 1886 gold was discovered in South Africa. The gold mines turned out to be the richest in the world. People started building a town near the gold fields. They called the town Johannesburg. Today it is one of the biggest and most modern towns in Africa. South Africa now produces three-quarters of the world's gold, after which comes Russia, Canada, the USA and Australia.

In 1896 an American Indian discovered gold in a creek near the Klondike River in Canada. Within a year a new town housing 4,000 people had been built. A year later this had grown to 30,000, as fortune-hunters arrived from all over Canada and the USA.

There is gold in Britain – royal wedding rings have been made of gold 'panned' in Wales. You can even go panning for gold yourself in some Welsh rivers, but you usually have to spend a very long time washing sand before you find even a tiny grain of gold!

There is still gold fever today in South Africa, but it's not about digging for gold. The most popular 'soap opera' on South African TV is called 'Egoli – Place of gold'. It's mostly about people who live in Johannesburg – the city built on gold.

• **Test 2a Reading non-fiction** •

Gold!

The questions on the next four pages are all about the passage *Gold!* When you are thinking of the answers, you can look back at the piece any time you want.

1 Write the names of **four** countries in which gold has been mined.

✎ (a) _____

(b) _____

(c) _____

(d) _____

2 Write the names of **two** kinds of gold coins.

✎ (a) _____

(b) _____

3 Write a list of the things we are told that gold is used to make.

✎ _____   _____

_____   _____

_____   _____

_____   _____

4 What time would you turn on the TV if you wanted to watch 'Egoli – Place of Gold'?

✎ _____

© O.U.P. 1996

PAGE TOTAL

5 What programmes would you see if you watched CCV television from 4.40 to 6.00?

✎ --

----

6 Why are aircraft windscreens covered with gold?

✎ --

----

7 Which word is used to mean a mixture of metals?

✎ --

8 Which word is used to describe the process by which gold is extracted from sand?

✎ --

9 Which country would you be in if you were near a gold mine and you were watching 'Egoli – Place of Gold' on TV?

✎ --

10 Name **two** towns or cities which have gold fields near them.

✎ **(a)** --

(b) --

© O.U.P. 1996

PAGE TOTAL

11 The text mentions **two** parts of the body which might have gold in or on them. What are they?

✎ **(a)** _____

(b) _____

12 What do we use today instead of gold coins?

✎ _____

_____

_____

13 Which word **best** describes the modern method of gold extraction?

✎ _____

14 How has gold mining changed over the past 100 years?

✎ _____

_____

_____

_____

© O.U.P. 1996

PAGE TOTAL

Precious Objects
Jewellery, Charms and Medals

Jewellery

Throughout the ages people have worn jewellery. Some is worn on the body: earrings, finger and toe rings, bracelets and necklaces. Other types are fastened to clothing: brooches, buckles, pins and badges.

Ornament

The most widespread use of jewellery is as simple decoration. The word itself hints that jewellery should contain precious jewels, but many items that people wear are made from inexpensive materials like seeds, bone, wood and plastic.

Symbols of status

Jewellery may also be worn to send a message about the wearer. In Canada, engineers may wear an iron ring to show they have qualified. Campaigners may wear a badge saying what cause they support. In many cultures, married people choose to wear a ring, although the design of the ring and the finger on which it is worn may vary. A monarch may have splendid jewellery to indicate the importance of his or her position.

The British Crown Jewels: *Saint Edward's crown*, the lower part of which was used in the coronation of King Edward in 1042; the *Orb*, carried in the monarch's hand; and the *Royal Sceptre*, containing the Cullinan diamond – 'The Star of Africa'.

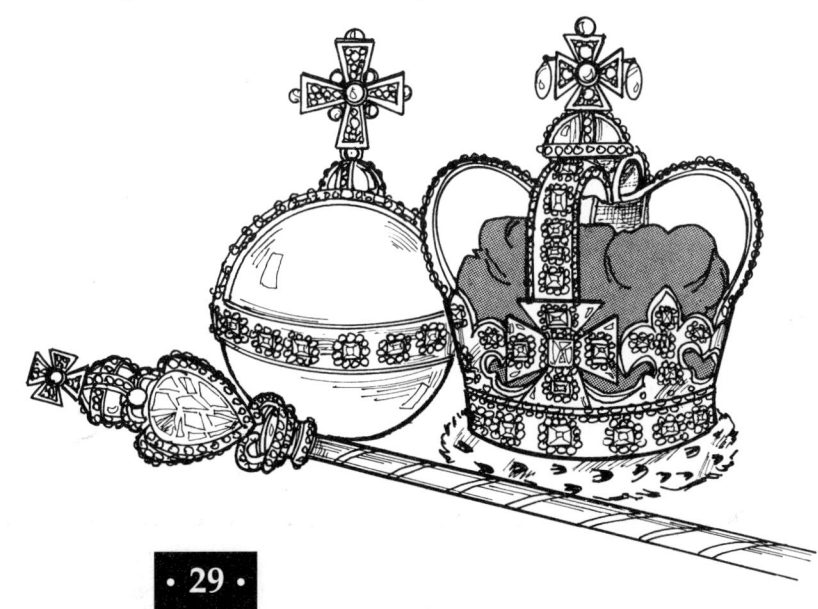

© O.U.P. 1996

Symbols of wealth

Precious jewels can be made up into jewellery and worn to show people how wealthy the wearer is.

In some cultures precious jewellery is worn in order to keep it safe. In others, people are too afraid to wear their wealth, in case they are attacked and robbed, so it is locked away in bank vaults and treated as an investment.

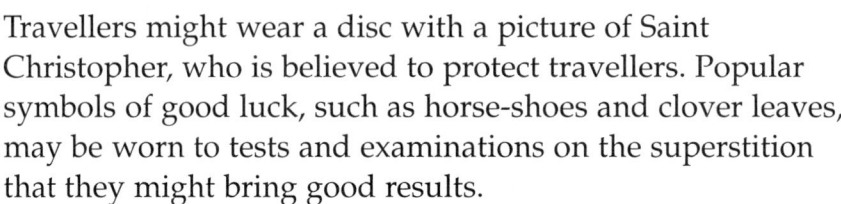

Special properties

Throughout the ages, people have worn jewellery as amulets, which means they thought the jewellery would protect them in some way.

Travellers might wear a disc with a picture of Saint Christopher, who is believed to protect travellers. Popular symbols of good luck, such as horse-shoes and clover leaves, may be worn to tests and examinations on the superstition that they might bring good results.

A more practical example is the medical identity bracelet, giving health information in case of emergency.

Lucky Charms

Abracadabra

The magical arrangement of these letters was, for the Romans, a protection against disease, misfortune and death. It was worn in the Middle Ages to keep the wearer safe from plague and its popularity revived during the Great Plague of 1665.

Today, some stage and TV magicians still say 'Abracadabra' as the 'magic word' to make a trick work.

Hei-Tiki

Traditionally, the Maori people of New Zealand carve these out of jade, although today you can buy plastic tikis. They are worn around the neck for good luck and to ward off evil influences.

Amongst Maori families these charms can be valuable heirlooms, handed down through generations and absorbing the virtues and good qualities of their successive owners.

© O.U.P. 1996

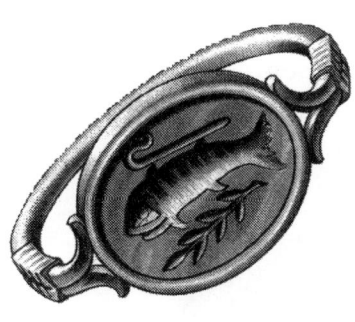

Fish

As well as being one of the ancient signs of the zodiac, the fish was the symbol of the Egyptian goddess of the floods of the River Nile, which brought fertility and prosperity to the Nile Delta.

The symbol was adopted by early Christians and used on rings, partly as a declaration of faith, but also as a charm to promote success and happiness.

Crescent

Thousands of years ago in Eastern countries, crescents were worn as a safeguard against danger. The crescent probably derives from the image of the moon in partial eclipse.

As horse-shoes were developed by the Greeks and Romans, their similarity of shape to the crescent caused them to be regarded as lucky. Even today, many houses in this country have a 'lucky' horse-shoe hanging up on a wall.

Medals

The purpose of a medal is to mark an outstanding deed. People value a medal because the deed itself is worth remembering, not because the medal is valuable in itself.

The earliest medals were laurel leaves, made by the ancient Greeks for their heroes. The ancient Greeks and Romans soon began making medals out of metal, because it was a more permanent reminder of an important event.

Many governments award medals to people who have performed a great deed for their country. Soldiers can win medals for bravery. Other people, such as politicians, may receive medals for having made peace. Scientists who make important discoveries may be honoured with a medal for having brought glory to their country.

Organisations who do rescue work, such as the police, may award a medal to people who risk their lives to save others. A medal is given as part of the prize at many types of competitions, including the Olympic Games. Medals are also made to commemorate an important event, such as a new ruler or leader, or a major victory in war.

Order of El Nahda, Hedjaz
A military medal from
the Middle East

© O.U.P. 1996

Victoria Cross, *United Kingdom*
The 'VC', awarded to soldiers, sailors and airmen in military service, was instituted by Queen Victoria in 1856 for 'conspicuous bravery ... in the presence of the enemy'. The medals were originally made from captured Russian guns.

Order of the Legion of Honour, *France*
Instituted by Napoleon in 1802, this medal is the highest French honour. It is given as a reward for service to France either in the army or as a civilian.

Congressional Medal of Honor (Army), *USA*
The highest award in the United States. Awarded, since 1862, in several different civil and militery versions for a range of achievements including bravery and working for world peace.

The Order of the Rising Sun, *Japan*
Although this is not the highest honour in Japan, it is one of the oldest Japanese medals. This civil and military medal was instituted by the Mikado (Emperor) of Japan, Mutsuhito, in 1876. It is awarded in eight classes of merit.

The Waterloo Medal, *United Kingdom*
Unlike the other medals shown, this medal was awarded just once to all British men who fought at the Battle of Waterloo under the command of the Duke of Wellington in 1815.

© O.U.P. 1996

• Test 2b Reading non-fiction •

Precious Objects

The questions on the next four pages are all about the passage *Precious Objects – Jewellery, Charms and Medals.* When you are thinking of the answers, you can look back at the piece any time you want.

Draw a line under the correct answer when required.

Jewellery

1 Complete this chart which is based on information given in the first paragraph on page 29:

Jewellery worn on the body	Jewellery worn on clothes
Earrings	
Toe rings	
Necklaces	

2 What is the 'Star of Africa'?

The town of Johannesburg   a nugget of gold

a diamond   a sceptre

© O.U.P. 1996

PAGE
TOTAL

3 What does the word 'amulet' mean?

✎ -- ☐

-- ☐

Lucky Charms

4 Which lucky charm is traditionally carved out of jade?

Abracadabra   Hei-Tiki   Crescent   Fish   ☐

5 Which lucky charm is supposed to protect you from the plague?

Abracadabra   Hei-Tiki   Crescent   Fish   ☐

6 Which **two** lucky charms might have been worn by people in Ancient Egypt?

Abracadabra   Hei-Tiki   Crescent   Fish   ☐
☐

7 Which lucky charm is most likely to be given by a father to his son?

Abracadabra   Hei-Tiki   Crescent   Fish   ☐

8 Which lucky charm has always been linked to wealth and success?

Abracadabra   Hei-Tiki   Crescent   Fish   ☐

© O.U.P. 1996

PAGE TOTAL

9 Which lucky charms were first worn by people who did not live in Britain?

Abracadabra   Hei-Tiki   Crescent   Fish

10 In the passage about Lucky Charms, why are the words 'lucky' and 'magic word' in inverted commas?

✎ _____

_____

_____

Medals

11 Write a list of the medals shown in the order in which they were first awarded. Write the name of the earliest medal first:

Medal number 1: _____

Medal number 2: _____

Medal number 3: _____

Medal number 4: _____

Medal number 5: _____

12 Which medal was given to the Duke of Wellington's soldiers?

Victoria Cross   Waterloo Medal   Rising Sun

Legion of Honour   Medal of Honor

© O.U.P. 1996

PAGE TOTAL

13   Which **two** medals are British?

Victoria Cross   Waterloo Medal   Rising Sun

Legion of Honour   Medal of Honor

☐

14   Which medals can be given to civilians (people not in the army, navy or airforce)?

Victoria Cross   Waterloo Medal   Rising Sun

Legion of Honour   Medal of Honor

☐
☐

15   Which medals are for military use only?

Victoria Cross   Waterloo Medal   Rising Sun

Legion of Honour   Medal of Honor

☐

16   Which medals are the highest honours that can be given by a country to a civilian?

Victoria Cross   Waterloo Medal   Rising Sun

Legion of Honour   Medal of Honor

☐

17   The words 'FOR VALOUR' are on the Victoria Cross and the word 'VALOR' is on the Medal of Honor. 'Valour' and 'valor' are two different spellings of the same word. What do you think the word 'valour' or 'valor' means?

✎ _____

_____

_____

☐

© O.U.P. 1996

PAGE TOTAL

18 Can you find another word in the passage about medals that is spelled in two different ways?

✎ --- ☐

19 Why do you think 'valour' and 'valor' are spelled differently?

✎ ---

--- ☐

--- ☐

20 Many medals are made in gold or silver, but the Victoria Cross is made out of gun-metal, which is quite cheap. Why do you think a cheap metal was used for the highest award for bravery?

✎ ---

--- ☐

--- ☐

--- ☐

© O.U.P. 1996

PAGE
TOTAL

The Dragon of Death

In a faraway, faraway forest
lies a treasure of infinite worth,
but guarding it closely forever
looms a being as old as the earth.

Its body is big as a boulder
and armoured with shimmering scales,
even the mountaintops tremble
when it thrashes its seven great tails.

Its eyes tell a story of terror,
they gleam with an angry red flame
as it timelessly watches its riches,
and the dragon of death is its name.

Its teeth are far sharper than daggers,
they can tear hardest metal to shreds.
It has seven mouths filled with these weapons,
for its neck swells to seven great heads.

Each head is as fierce as the other,
each head breathes a fiery breath,
and any it touches must perish,
set ablaze by the dragon of death.

All who have foolishly stumbled
on the dragon of death's golden cache
remain evermore in that forest,
nothing left of their bodies but ash.

Jack Prelutsky

© O.U.P. 1996

The Dragon of Death

The questions on the next two pages are all about the poem *The Dragon of Death*. When you are thinking of the answers, you can look back at the poem any time you want.

Draw a line under the correct answer when required.

1 What is the dragon guarding?

a forest   treasure   a boulder   a flame ☐

2 How many heads does the dragon have?

one   three   five   seven ☐

3 How big do you think the dragon is?

as big as a mouse   as big as a goat

as big as an elephant   as big as a horse ☐

4 Which word in the poem rhymes with 'tails'?

✎ _____ ☐

5 What happens to people who find the treasure?

They get burned up.   They run away.

They get rich.   They have to fight the dragon. ☐

© O.U.P. 1996

PAGE TOTAL

6 Can you name **three** things which the dragon can use as weapons?

✎ **(a)** --

(b) --

□

(c) --

□

7 In the last verse, the word **'cache'** is used. What do you think the word 'cache' means?

A pile of money.   A seat.

□

Something hidden.   A metal box.

□

8 Why do you think the poem is called 'The Dragon of Death'?

✎ --

□

© O.U.P. 1996

PAGE TOTAL

Golden Glories

The buttercup is like a golden cup,
The marigold is like a golden frill,
The daisy with a golden eye looks up,
And golden spreads the flag beside the rill,
And gay and golden nods the daffodil;

The gorsey common swells a golden sea,
The cowslip hangs a head of golden tips,
And golden drips the honey which the bee
Sucks from sweet hearts of flowers and stores and sips.

Christina Rossetti
(born 1830, died 1894)

Glossary:
rill –   a little river
gorsey –   covered in gorse bushes
common – a large area of land

© O.U.P. 1996

• Test 3b Reading poetry • Time started :

Time finished :

Golden Glories

The questions on the next two pages are all about the poem *Golden Glories*. When you are thinking of the answers, you can look back at the poem any time you want.

Draw a line under the correct answer when required.

1 In the poem the writer is talking about lots of different

insects   gold   flowers   flags   ☐

2 Which flower is described as 'like a golden frill'?

buttercup   marigold   daisy   daffodil   ☐

3 What colour do you think the flowers are on 'the gorsey common'?

red   yellow   green   orange   ☐

4 Which insect is mentioned in the poem?

✎ _____   ☐

5 Look at the whole poem and find the names of **five** flowers.

✎ **(a)** _____

(b) _____

(c) _____

(d) _____   ☐

(e) _____   ☐

6 Which word in the poem rhymes with '**sips**'?

✎ _____   ☐

© O.U.P. 1996

PAGE TOTAL

7 Which **two** words in the poem rhyme with **'frill'**?

(a) _____

(b) _____

8 What time of year is the writer describing?

Spring   Summer   Autumn   Winter

9 How can you tell what time of year it is?

_____

_____

10 The word **'flag'** has many meanings. Which meaning of flag do you think the author is using in the fourth line of this poem?

A piece of cloth fixed to a pole   A leafy plant growing on
or a rope, used as an emblem   moist ground.
or signal.

The quill-feather on a bird's wing.   A flat slab of stone used for paving.

11 Why do you think the poem is called 'Golden Glories'?

_____

_____

_____

12 Why do you think the writer uses the word **'swells'** in the line:
'The gorsey common swells a golden sea'?

_____

_____

_____

© O.U.P. 1996

PAGE
TOTAL

• Test 4a Story writing • | Time started [:] | Time finished [:]

Story writing

Here are three ideas for a story. Choose one of them as the starting point for your story writing. You can use the box below to plan your story and you can use the boxes opposite to make notes about the ideas in your story. (You do not have to use the boxes if you don't want to.) You can spend about 10 to 15 minutes planning your story.

 **(a)** You find a very old book in the school library. At home you open the book to look at it, but you notice that something is hidden in the spine of the book. You pull it out and find that it appears to be an old map. Write a story about the old map and where it leads you.

 **(b)** In your local newspaper there is a report which says that a mining company is going to look for gold in the field next to your house! One of your friends suggests that you could look for gold in your back garden. Write a story about digging for gold in your garden.

 **(c)** A present like a gold brooch or a pearl necklace may cost a lot of money, but sometimes a present is special for other reasons. Write a story about a present and the person it is given to.

Your Notes:

© O.U.P. 1996

Story planning notes

Title

Setting (Where and when does it take place?)

Characters (Who are they? How old are they?)

What starts the story?

What happens next?

How does the story end?

© O.U.P. 1996

• Test 4b Letter writing •

| Time started | : |
| Time finished | : |

Letter writing

Here are three ideas for a letter. Choose one of them as the starting point for your letter writing. You can use the box below to plan your letter and you can use the boxes opposite to make notes about the main points you want to make in your letter. (You do not have to use the boxes if you don't want to.) You can spend 5 to 10 minutes planning your letter.

(a) You catch a bus to get to school, but every day for the past two weeks, the bus has been late. Your teacher has had to mark you late and has asked you to try to get to school on time. Write to the bus company about the late buses.

(b) In your local newspaper there is a letter which says that young people today are a disgrace. Write a reply to the paper explaining why this is not true.

(c) Last week you saw an advert in a magazine for a brilliant teeshirt. You filled in the coupon and sent the money. This week the teeshirt has arrived, but it is too small and the picture on it is not at all like the one in the advert. Write a letter about the teeshirt.

Your Notes:

© O.U.P. 1996

Letter planning notes

Who is it to?

How do you start your letter?

What points do you want to make?

What do you want the company (or the newspaper, or someone else) to do?

How do you end your letter?

© O.U.P. 1996

• Test 5a Spelling •

Treasures of Britain – 1

1

The Hyde Abbey Staff

Not all treasures are made of gold or silver or precious

jewels. Some of the .... treasures in ☐

our country are valuable .... they are ☐

so special that they could never be .... ☐

The Hyde Abbey Staff or 'crosier' was found in 1783,

when people were digging on the .... ☐

of Hyde Abbey, Winchester. When .... ☐

is made a Bishop or an Abbot in the Christian Church,

they are given a staff like this as a .... ☐

of their office. It is made to look like the crook used by a

.... to catch the sheep. ☐

The top of this staff is made to look like grapes and vine

.... It was made in the early 13th ☐

century. Although it looks as though it is gold, it is

actually made of copper, ... with ☐

a very thin layer of gold. It is valuable because it

is .... and very old. ☐

© O.U.P. 1996

See page 61 for guide sheet.

PAGE
TOTAL

• Test 5b Spelling •

Treasures of Britain – 2

2

The Alfred Jewel

This famous jewel was found in 1693 near the Isle of

Athelney in Somerset. We .... that   ☐

King Alfred .... to this place in the   ☐

year 878 when he was being hard ....   ☐

by the armies of the .... Danes. The   ☐

jewel .... dates from around this time.   ☐

The setting is made of gold and the .... ,   ☐

which is believed to show King Alfred himself, is made of

thin gold wire with enamel .... between   ☐

the wires. Around the .... of the   ☐

setting are old English words which ....   ☐

'Alfred had me made'. The jewel is now in the

Ashmolean .... in Oxford.   ☐

See page 62 for guide sheet.

© O.U.P. 1996

PAGE
TOTAL

• Test 5c Spelling •

Treasures of Britain – 3

3

The Lindisfarne Gospels

This beautiful book contains the four books of the

Bible known as the gospels .... to ☐

Matthew, Mark, Luke and John. The book is in Latin,

the .... of the Romans. The whole ☐

book was written and .... by hand at ☐

the end of the 7th .... About three ☐

hundred years later, a .... into ☐

English was written between the lines of Latin.

Eadfrith, Bishop of Lindisfarne, had the book made

in .... of Saint Cuthbert who ☐

was his .... as bishop. ☐

The manuscript is richly illustrated. Many coloured

inks were used to .... the ☐

artwork. The monks who worked on the book

often made .... designs around ☐

the .... letters of a new chapter, ☐

as you can see in the picture.

© O.U.P. 1996

See page 62 for guide sheet.

PAGE TOTAL

• Test 6 Handwriting •

Time started :

Time finished :

Read this poem about books, written by John Kitching.

Then copy the poem in the space below.

You can use a pen or a pencil.

☞ Write in your normal handwriting.

☞ Write as carefully and neatly as you can.

☞ Join the letters where you are supposed to.

Books

Believe the golden stories in your head

And all the golden stories that you read,

For what you deeply feel

As truth is much more real

Than all that can be counted, cold and dead.

✎ --

© O.U.P. 1996

PAGE TOTAL

• ANSWERS •

Answers to Test 1a
Reading fiction: pp 10 – 13
Midas

The first eleven questions are concerned with literal understanding of the story.

1 Midas was king of

Phrygia (1 mark)

2 Dionysus warned that the golden touch would bring Midas

sorrow (1 mark)

3 When Midas came in shouting 'Gold! Gold!', the queen thought he was

crazy (1 mark)

4 Midas turned his dog into gold because

Midas forgot he had the golden touch (1 mark)

5 The Princess turned to gold because

she touched her father's neck (1 mark)

6 How did Midas lose the golden touch?

he bathed in a river (1 mark)

7 Who came back to life again?

the Princess and the dog (1 mark)

8 How much gold did Midas want at the beginning of the story?

lots (1 mark)

9 How much gold did Midas want at the end of the story?

none at all (1 mark)

10 Where do you think this story was first told?

ancient Greece (1 mark)

11 ✔ = things turned to gold
✗ = things not turned to gold

his throne	✔	his dinner	✔
his horse	✗	his clothes	✗
his daughter	✔	his wine cup	✔
his wife	✗	his cat	✗
his dog	✔	his bed	✗
his table	✗	his knife	✔
his hair	✗	his jewellery	✗
		his wine	✔

(1 mark for 13 or 14 correct; 2 for all 15 correct)

About the characters:

12 Why do you think Midas described the golden touch as a 'deadly curse'?

1 mark for an answer which mentions *either* that the golden touch turned people (and animals) into gold *or* that Midas would soon be dead because he could not eat (or drink). 3 marks if both reasons given. (1-3 marks)

13 Which of these words best describes what Midas felt about gold at the beginning of the story?

greed (2 marks)

14 What kind of person do you think the Queen was?

1 mark for one or two appropriate words, such as *sensible / down to earth / cautious*. 3 marks for a more complex answer using full sentences and giving a description based on the Queen's words and actions in the story. (1-3 marks)

How the story is written:

15 Which word in the first paragraph of the story means 'clever' and 'sensible'?

wise (1 mark)

16 Which two words describe the voice of Dionysus?

deep (1 mark if *both*
booming words are written)

17 Why do you think Midas said 'This is serious'?

Give 2 marks for an answer which clearly implies that Midas realised he would soon die if he could not eat.

Opinions and appreciation of the story as a whole

18 Did you like this story? Yes/No

Either Yes or No is acceptable because the marks are given for how well the answer justifies yes or no. Give 1 mark if the answer gives any valid reason justifying yes or no. Give 2 marks if the answer gives at least two *different* reasons justifying yes or no.

19 Would you like to be given the golden touch? Yes / No

Either Yes or No is acceptable because the marks are given for how well the answer justifies yes or no. Give 1 mark if the answer gives any valid reason justifying yes or no. Give 2 marks if the answer gives at least two *different* reasons justifying yes or no.

20 Meaning of 'having the golden touch'.

Give 2 marks for an answer which indicates that the expression is used to mean that everything they do is successful or profitable. Do not give a mark for a simple explanation such as 'everything they touch turns to gold' unless this is also further explained.

Total .... out of 30

Answers to Test 1b
Reading fiction: pp 18 – 21
Interest on Ten Shillings

The first ten questions are concerned with understanding the events and the factual details of the story.

1 Men worked at the gold mine with

picks and shovels   (1 mark)

2 When Allan bought the mine, he thought the price he had paid for it was

small   (1 mark)

3 After working on the mine for three months, Allan thought the mine was

a waste of money   (1 mark)

4 When Allan emptied his purse and looked at his money, he had

less than one pound   (1 mark)

5 When Allan couldn't find the missing coin he was

annoyed   (1 mark)

6 How big was the biggest nugget of gold?

like an apple   (1 mark)

7 How much was half a sovereign?

ten shillings (50p)   (1 mark)

8 What did Harry think was odd when he picked up the stone?

It was heavy.   (1 mark)

9 How much was Allan's gold worth?

£1250   (1 mark)

10 Which book is the story taken from?

Allan's Wife and Other Tales   (1 mark)

Question 11 is concerned with the sequence of events in the story.

11 The correct order of events in the story is:

1. Allan bought a gold mine.
2. Allan dropped a half-sovereign into the mine.
3. Allan and Harry went to look for the lost coin.
4. Harry pulled out a stone.
5. Allan found the stone was gold.
6. Allan sold the gold mine.

Give 1 mark for getting the first and last events in the correct place. Give 2 marks for a completely correct list.

Questions 12 to 14 are about the main character and his feelings.

12 Why do you think Allan believed the gold mine was worth buying?

1 mark if the answer indicates that he knew the previous owner had made a fortune from it.

13 The activity Allan liked doing most.

Give 1 mark if *Looking at the mountains and valleys* is underlined.

What is there in the story which helps you to decide which activity he liked best?

1 mark for a simple explanation, like 'He walked to the top of a hill'. or 'He liked looking at the mountains'. 2 marks for an explanation which clearly indicates that he was often disgusted or fed up with mining *and* that he found the scenery beautiful, or that he left his work to look at the scenery.

14 What kind of person do you think Allan Quartermain was?

1 mark for two or more words from the story which simply describe Allan, such as: *a hunter / angry / annoyed / astonished / excited*. 3 marks for a longer description which contains two or more appropriate words not in the story, such as: *brave / adventurous / daring / bold / an outdoor type / a risk-taker*.

Questions 15 to 17 are looking at how story is written.

15 Which word on the second page of the story means 'a large amount of money'?

fortune   (1 mark)

16 Four words in the story which tell you about Allan's feelings at various times.

Possible answers: *disgust / angry / annoyance / astonishment / thrills / excitement / trembling.*
1 mark for two possible answers.
2 marks for four possible answers.

17 Why did the writer choose to use the word 'crisis'?

1 mark if the answer indicates that Allan was about to run out of money / had no money left / could not afford any more food or wages.

Questions 18 to 20 are concerned with your child's opinions, which represent the extent of their understanding and appreciation of the story as a whole.

18 Did you like story? Yes / No

Either Yes or No is acceptable because the marks are given for how well the answer justifies yes or no.
1 mark if the answer gives any valid reason justifying yes or no.
3 marks if the answer gives *two* valid reasons justifying yes or no.

19 Why do you think the title of this story is *The Interest on Ten Shillings* ?

1 mark for mentioning that the story is about a lost ten shillings.
3 marks if the answer refers to interest in its financial sense, or clearly explains that the process of losing the half-sovereign led directly to discovering the gold, or contrasts in terms of value the loss of the coin with the finding of the gold nuggets.

20 Would you like to dig for gold like Allan Quartermain? Explain.

Give 1 mark for any reasonable explanation for either yes or no.

Total .... out of 30

Answers to Test 2a
Reading non fiction: pp 26 –28
Gold!

1 Write the names of four countries in which gold has been mined.

Lydia / Australia / South Africa / Russia / Canada / USA / Britain *or* Wales (if both Britain *and* Wales are written, count them as just one correct answer).
1 mark for any three correct answers.
2 marks for four correct answers.

2 Write the names of two kinds of gold coins.

sovereigns / krugerrands
1 mark for each correct answer.

3 Write a list of the things that we are told that gold is used to make.

One of: coins *or* sovereigns *or* krugerrands. One of: gold leaf *or* book edges *or* picture frames. One of: fillings *or* cappings (teeth) / (electrical) contacts / aircraft windscreens / rings.
1 mark for at least 3 correct answers.
2 marks for at least 4 correct answers.

4 Time to watch 'Egoli'.

1 mark for 6.00 or 6 o'clock.

5 What programmes would you see if you watched CCV television from 4.40 to 6.00?

1 mark for *Days of our Lives*.
1 mark for *The Bold and the Beautiful*.

6 Why are aircraft windscreens covered with gold?

1 mark for cutting down glare.
1 mark for preventing icing.

7 Word used to mean a mixture of metals.

1 mark for alloying.
2 marks for alloy.

8 Word used to describe the process by which gold is extracted from sand.

1 mark for pan or panned.
3 marks for panning.

9 Country to watch 'Egoli' on TV?

1 mark for Africa.
2 marks for South Africa.

10 Name two towns or cities which have gold fields near them.

Melbourne / Johannesburg / Klondike
1 mark for any one correct answer.
2 marks for any two correct answers.

11 Two parts of the body (mentioned in text) which might have gold on or in them.

1 mark for teeth (or tooth).
1 mark for fingers (or finger).

12 What do we use today instead of gold coins?

2 marks for paper money (or paper).

13 Which word best describes the modern method of gold extraction?

3 marks for chemical *or* chemically.

14 How has gold mining changed over the past 100 years?

1 mark if the explanation contrasts panning and/or individual digging with deep mining. 2 marks if explosives and/or heavy machinery are mentioned in contrast to digging or panning by hand. 3 marks if the explanation clearly describes how modern mining is an industrial process undertaken by large mining companies in contrast to individual manual production of 100 years ago.

Total .... out of 30

Answers to Test 2b
Reading non fiction: pp 33 – 37
Precious Objects

Jewellery

1 Complete this chart which is based on information given in the first paragraph on page 29:

Jewellery worn on the body	Jewellery worn on clothes
earrings	brooches
finger rings	buckles
toe rings	pins
bracelets	badges
necklaces	

Words do not have to be in any order, but have to be in the correct column. 1 mark for a correctly completed chart.

2 What is the 'Star of Africa'?

a diamond (1 mark)

3 What does the word 'amulet' mean?

Give 2 marks for any definition which includes (a) that it is worn on the body, and (b) that is is a charm or protection. Both (a) and (b) must be included for a correct answer.

Lucky Charms

4 Which lucky charm is traditionally carved out of jade?

Hei-Tiki (1 mark)

5 Which lucky charm is supposed to protect you from the plague?

Abracadabra (1 mark)

6 Which two lucky charms might have been worn by people in Ancient Egypt?

Crescent *and* Fish

Give 2 marks for both correct answers. (No marks for only one correct answer.)

7 Which lucky charm is most likely to be given by a father to his son?

Hei-Tiki (1 mark)

8 Which lucky charm has always been linked to wealth and success?

Fish (1 mark)

9 Which lucky charms were first worn by people who did not live in Britain?

| Abracadabra | Crescent |
| Hei-Tiki | Fish |

2 marks for all four answers. (No marks for anything less than all four.)

10 In the passage about Lucky Charms, why are the words 'lucky' and 'magic word' in inverted commas?

Give 3 marks for any answer that indicates that the inverted commas are used to imply irony, doubt or disagreement that the objects are lucky or magic.

Medals

11 List of the medals shown in the order in which they were first awarded.

Medal number 1:	Order of the Legion of Honour
Medal number 2:	The Waterloo Medal
Medal number 3:	Victoria Cross
Medal number 4:	Congressional Medal of Honor
Medal number 5:	The Order of the Rising Sun

2 marks for a completely correct order.

12 Which medal was given to the Duke of Wellington's soldiers?

Waterloo Medal (1 mark)

13 Which two medals are British?

Waterloo Medal *and* Victoria Cross

1 mark for two correct answers.

14 Which medals can be given to civilians (people not in the army, navy or airforce)?

Legion of Honour
Medal of Honor
Rising Sun

2 marks for all three correct answers.

15 Which medals are for military use?

Victoria Cross *and* Waterloo Medal

1 mark for two correct answers.

16 Which medals are the highest honours that can be given by a country to a civilian?

Legion of Honour *and* Medal of Honor

1 mark for two correct answers.

17 The words 'FOR VALOUR' are on the Victoria Cross and the word 'VALOR' is on the Medal of Honor. 'Valour' and 'valor' are two different spellings of the same word. What do you think the word 'valour' or 'valor' means?

1 mark for any answer which clearly indicates: courage / bravery / risking life

18 Another word in the passage about medals that is spelled in two different ways?

1 mark for *Honour* / *Honor* (either word or both words)

19 Why do you think 'valour' and 'valor' are spelled differently?

2 marks for an answer which explains that 'valor' is an American (USA) or Latin (Roman) spelling. (No marks for an answer which says that words can have different spellings, but does not specifically mention the USA or America.)

20 Why do you think a cheap metal was used for the highest award for bravery?

2 marks for an answer which indicates that the value of the medal lies: in its rarity / in its prestige / in its honour, rather than in its worth as expensive metal. 1 additional mark for mentioning that the medals were originally made from captured enemy guns.

Total .... out of 30

Answers to Test 3a
Reading poetry: pp 39
The Dragon of Death

1 What is the dragon guarding?

treasure (1 mark)

2 How many heads does the dragon have?

seven (1 mark)

3 How big do you think the dragon is?

as big as an elephant (1 mark)

4 Which word in the poem rhymes with 'tails'?

scales (1 mark)

5 What happens to people who find the treasure?

They get burned up. (1 mark)

6 Can you name three things which the dragon can use as weapons?

tails / teeth / fiery (1 mark for 2 words)
breath (fire / flames) (2 marks for 3 words)

7 In the last verse, the word 'cache' is used. What do you think 'cache' means?

Something hidden. (2 marks)

8 Why do you think the poem is called 'The Dragon of Death'?

Give 1 mark for any answer which explains that anyone trying to get the treasure will be killed by the dragon.

Total .... out of 10

Answers to Test 3b
Reading poetry: pp 42 – 43
Golden Glories

1 In the poem the writer is talking about lots of different:

flowers (1 mark)

2 Which flower is described as 'like a golden frill'?

marigold (1 mark)

3 What colour do you think the flowers are on 'the gorsey common'?

yellow (1 mark)

4 Which insect is mentioned in the poem?

a bee (1 mark)

5 Look at the whole poem and find the names of five flowers.

buttercup / marigold / daisy / daffodil / gorse / cowslip
1 mark for any four correct names.
2 marks for five or six correct names.

6 Which word in the poem rhymes with 'sips'?

tips *or* drips (1 mark)

7 Which two words in the poem rhyme with 'frill'?

rill *and* daffodil
1 mark for each correct word.

8 What time of year is the writer describing?

Summer *or* Spring (1 mark)

9 How can you tell what time of year it is?

1 mark for an explanation that mentions flowers in bloom or the bee collecting nectar.

10 The word 'flag' has many meanings. Which meaning of flag do you think the author is using in the fourth line of this poem?

A leafy plant growing on moist ground. (3 marks)

11 Why do you think the poem is called 'Golden Glories'?

1 mark for an explanation that mentions flowers in bloom or the bee collecting nectar.
3 marks for indicating everything said in the poem can be a golden colour. (1-3 marks)

12 Why do you think the writer uses the word 'swells' in the line: 'The gorsey common swells a golden sea'?

1 mark for an answer which implies that either gorse or the sea can swell up high or can cover a wide area.
3 marks if the answer refers to the 'swell' of the sea or goes into relevant detail as to how the yellow flowers of the gorse cover such a wide area that they can look like the swelling waves of a golden sea. (1-3 marks)

Total .... out of 20

Assessing your pupils' reading using all the reading tests 1 to 3

➻ Fill in the scores for tests 1a and 1b, 2a and 2b, 3a and 3b in the first box on page 64.

➻ Add all the scores together to give an overall reading score out of a maximum of 150.

➻ Mark the total with a cross in the Reading Score column on the left of the National Curriculum Record.

➻ The band which the child's score is in indicates which National Curriculum Level the child has reached in reading.

• Marking Writing: Tests 4a & 4b •

The Writing Test at Key Stage 2 is trying to measure 'a growing ability to construct and convey meaning in written language matching style to audience and purpose'. This is not easy to understand – it is even less easy to do!

In assessing writing, it is impossible to set questions for which there is only one answer, as can happen in, for example, Maths. Assessing writing is all about making judgements and estimating a level. The following criteria represent a slight simplification of those provided for the KS2 test and should help you to get a fairly good idea of the pupils' writing ability, but do remember that the quality of a child's writing varies much more than does their reading, spelling or handwriting skills, and that judgements about writing are very personal.

Children's writing is assessed in three broad areas:

1) Purpose and organisation – How good are the child's ideas and how well has the child organised the ideas into a piece of writing?
2) Grammar – How correct is the child's use of written English?
3) Style – How well written is the child's piece of writing?

Use the following criteria to assess each pupil's writing. Then, find the Level with the description which best matches your perception of what each child has written. If you are not sure, look at the levels either side of the one which you think a child may have attained. Is the writing better than the description for the level below? Is the writing not as good as the description for the level above? Award only the marks for the level which you think best describes a child's writing.

1 Marks for Purpose and organisation

Level 1: Award 2 marks
Writing which is about the subject, makes sense but does not qualify for Level 2.

Level 2: Award 5 marks
Story Writing: A beginning to the story, more than one character, two or more events in the right order. Some description of the setting or the characters and some structure to the story.
Letter Writing: A simple but appropriate structure, e.g. it looks a bit like a letter. Some points made, but not really connected to present an argument.

Level 3: Award 7 marks
Writing includes details which add interest or humour or suspense.
Story Writing: Some detail in describing the setting or the characters. A simple ending to the story.
Letter Writing: A clear introduction. A series of points made, generally connected to present an argument.

Level 4: Award 10 marks
Events or points are logically related. There is a clear beginning, middle and end. Two or more paragraphs may be used to show different sections.
Story Writing: The characters clearly interact. There may be some direct or reported speech. The tone of the story implies that the writer knows it is being read by someone.
Letter Writing: An appropriate structure, e.g. it has the qualities and appearance of a letter. The main points

are clearly expressed and present a logical argument.

Level 5: Award 12 marks
Writing is well structured with a clear beginning, middle and end. Paragraphs are used correctly. There is a convincing ending to a clear plot or argument. Dialogue, action and description may be present.
Story Writing: Comments on the action and asides to the reader may be present. More than one simple plot may be present.
Letter Writing: A clear structure with different points linked (*for example / secondly / another point that*) and presenting a strong logical argument.

Level 6: Award 15 marks
Sequence and detail are used to keep the reader's interest. A clear theme may run through the piece. There is a confident use of writing conventions, such as paragraphs, direct speech (with speech marks) and reported speech.
Story Writing: There may be a clear relationship or conflict between characters. There may be an element of surprise. Several episodes may be linked.
Letter Writing: The main issues are covered, with observations and comments, and arranged in paragraphs which include organisational phrases e.g. *As there were so many problems...* or *In response to the writer's other point....* All the conventions of a well-structured letter should be present, as should a concluding paragraph which summarises or persuades with a strong final argument.

2 Marks for Grammar

Level 1: Award 1 mark
Some evidence of independent writing (i.e. not copying), but not qualifying for Level 2.

Level 2: Award 2 marks
At least two sentences with correct capital letters at the beginning and full stops (or question marks) at the end.

Level 3: Award 3 marks
At least half the sentences on the first page have capital letters at the beginning and full stops (or question marks) at the end.

Level 4: Award 5 marks
Consistent and logical use of tense (past, present, future where appropriate).
• Three-quarters of sentences on the first page must have correct capital letters/full stops (or question or exclamation marks).
• Basic punctuation, such as speech marks, question marks and exclamation marks, should be correct in at least 50% of all instances where punctuation is used.

Level 5: Award 6 marks
No more than two errors in capital letters/full stops (or question or exclamation marks) on the first page.
• Commas correctly used.
• Speech marks, question marks and exclamation marks should be correct in at least 75% of all instances.

Level 6: Award 7 marks
Sustained accurate punctuation, with a variety of sentence and clause length to help the reader.

3 Marks for Style

Level 1:
Style does not apply to Level 1.

Level 2: Award 2 marks
Some ideas in simple sentences.

Level 3: Award 3 marks
More complex sentences with words like and, but, so to link ideas. Some adjectives and adverbs.

Level 4: Award 5 marks
Language which clearly sounds 'written' rather than spoken.
• Ideas connected with phrases such as, *when, if, although, so as to....*
• More complex detail, such as, *a shiny black car... a strong wooden box...*
Letter writing: Appropriate structures such as, *I am writing to reply to...*

Level 5: Award 7 marks
A variety of sentences and vocabulary written in standard English (except where dialect or slang is clearly used in speech).
• Meaning is clear and the whole passage (except for speech) is in a written style of English, clearly different from normal speech.

Level 6: Award 8 marks
Precise and varied use of written language.
• Well-chosen and varied verbs, e.g. *rushed / ambled / slid rather than went.*
• Words organised into sequences to give effect, such as *The whips cracked, the horses' hooves thudded and we sped through the dark....* Similes, e.g. *as green as grass,* and metaphors may be used.

Assessing pupils' writing using writing tests 4a and 4b

•◇ Story writing and Letter writing are assessed in levels, using the guidance above.

•◇ If the levels are not the same, the *higher* level gives a better indication of a pupil's potential, and thus gives a pointer as to where any weakness in writing may lie.

•◇ You can fill in the scores for tests 4a and 4b on a copy of the National Curriculum Record on page 64, and add the two scores together to give an overall Test 4 score out of a maximum of 60. When scores for spelling and handwriting are added, an overall writing score can be obtained.

• Answers to Spelling Tests 5a / 5b / 5c •

Test 5a – Spelling 1: Page 48

1.	greatest	6.	symbol	Give one mark for each correct answer:	
2.	because	7.	shepherd		
3.	replaced	8.	leaves		
4.	site	9.	covered		
5.	someone	10.	beautiful	**Score for Test 5a:** _____	

Test 5b – Spelling 2: Page 49

11.	know	16.	portrait	Give one mark for each correct answer:	
12.	retreated	17.	paint .		
13.	pressed	18.	edge		
14.	invading	19.	mean		
15.	probably	20.	Museum	**Score for Test 5b:** _____	

Test 5c – Spelling 3: Page 50

21.	according	26.	honour	Give one mark for each correct answer:	
22.	language	27.	predecessor		
23.	decorated	28.	illuminate		
24.	century	29.	elaborate		
25.	translation	30.	initial	**Score for Test 5c:** _____	

Total Test Score (all 3 tests): _____

Assessing pupils' spelling using all three spelling tests

Use this table to find your pupils' National Curriculum Spelling Levels.

Total Test Score (out of 30)	Spelling Level
1 – 2 *1-2*	1
3 – 7 *3*	2
8 – 15 *4-5*	3
16 – 21 *6-7*	4
22 – 27 *8-9*	5
28 – 30 *10*	6

Fill in the scores for tests 5a, 5b and 5c in the 3 boxes on page 64.

Add all the scores together, then divide the total by 2 to give an overall spelling score out of a maximum of 15.

• Dictation Scripts for Spelling Tests •

Instructions for Spelling Tests

❶ Pages 61 and 62 contain the scripts that you need to read to your pupils for the spelling (dictation) tests.

❷ Read the following to the pupils, changing the wording if appropriate:

I am going to read this to you. The version in your book has some words missing. You can follow as I read it, but don't write any words in yet.

❸ Read the passage.

Now I'll read it again. I'll tell you the missing words and I want you to write them in the gaps. If you're not sure how to spell the missing word, just write down the letters that you think might be right.

❹ Read the passage. Pause at each missing word, giving plenty of time for the pupils to write the spelling.

❺ Any of the above instructions can be repeated or changed at any time. Encourage the children, but do not give clues to spelling, such as *'What letter does it start with?'*, *'Are you sure that's right?'* or *'Is there something missing?'*

Test 5a Dictation Script – Spelling 1: page 48

Treasures of Britain – 1

The Hyde Abbey Staff

Not all treasures are made of gold or silver or precious jewels. Some of the **greatest** treasures in our country are valuable **because** they are so special that they could never be **replaced.**

The Hyde Abbey Staff or 'crosier' was found in 1783, when people were digging on the **site** of Hyde Abbey, Winchester. When **someone** is made a Bishop or an Abbot in the Christian Church, they are given a staff like this as a **symbol** of their office. It is made to look like the crook used by a **shepherd** to catch the sheep.

The top of this staff is made to look like grapes and vine **leaves.** It was made in the early 13th century. Although it looks as though it is gold, it is actually made of copper, **covered** with a very thin layer of gold. It is valuable because it is **beautiful** and very old.

• Dictation Scripts for Spelling Tests •

Treasures of Britain – 2

The Alfred Jewel

This famous jewel was found in 1693 near the Isle of Athelney in Somerset. We **know** that King Alfred **retreated** to this place in the year 878 when he was being hard **pressed** by the armies of the **invading** Danes. The jewel **probably** dates from around this time.

The setting is made of gold and the **portrait,** which is believed to show King Alfred himself, is made of thin gold wire with enamel **paint** between the wires. Around the **edge** of the setting are old English words which **mean** 'Alfred had me made'. The jewel is now in the Ashmolean **Museum** in Oxford.

Treasures of Britain – 3

The Lindisfarne Gospels

This beautiful book contains the four books of the Bible known as the gospels **according** to Matthew, Mark, Luke and John. The book is in Latin, the **language** of the Romans. The whole book was written and **decorated** by hand at the end of the 7th **century.** About three hundred years later, a **translation** into English was written between the lines of Latin.

Eadfrith, Bishop of Lindisfarne, had the book made in **honour** of Saint Cuthbert who was his **predecessor** as bishop.

The manuscript is richly illustrated. Many coloured inks were used to **illuminate** the artwork. The monks who worked on the book often made **elaborate** designs around the **initial** letters of a new chapter, as you can see in the picture.

The examples below can be used as 'quick' criteria for assessing the National Curriculum Level of children's handwriting.

- *Look at the example for Level 1. If the child's writing is better than this, but not as good as the example for Level 3, then award* **3 marks.**

- *If the child's writing is better than the example for Level 3, but not as good as the example for Level 5 then award* **7 marks.**

- *If the child's writing is as good as, or better than, the example for level 5 then award* **8 marks.**

- *If the child's writing is as good as Level 6, award* **10 marks.**

The written descriptions below are a summary of the National Curriculum Guidelines – these may be helpful if your pupils have learned a different style from those in the examples. The particular handwriting style children use is not a relevant criterion for assessment purposes. What is important is the *quality* of the handwriting, whatever style it is in.

Level 1 example

loHer bgheob9b.
A Church was bvilt oh the
plb ce where he bieb.

Level 3 example

On the 17th March it was st patrick
day. He was borned in wales. his father
was Roman. A.D. 389 - A.D. 461. st patrick
was on the beach.

Level 5 example

On Sheilas birthday her Daddy gave
her a very unusual present he took her
out into the garden and gave her a

Level 6 example

Autumn is one of the most interesting seasons for
trees. They often change colour and suffer from the loss
of leaves. The buds begin to appear; and one can generally

Written Descriptions of Levels
Level 1
Some recognisable letters
1 mark
Level 2
Letters generally formed correctly, with upper case (ABC) or lower case (abc) used consistently
3 marks
Level 3
Beginnings of clear legible writing, showing some ability to join letters
5 marks
Level 4
More fluent writing which is clear and legible/mostly joined letters/regular spacing and size
7 marks
Level 5
Clear, legible, neat in a cursive style
8 marks
Level 6
Mature, clear, legible, neat in a cursive style
10 marks

READING
Write how many you scored in each test.

WRITING
Write how many you scored in each test.

FICTION 1A — [/30]

FICTION 1B — [/30]

NON-FICTION 2A — [/30]

NON-FICTION 2A — [/30]

POETRY 3A — [/10]

POETRY 3B — [/20]

READING TOTAL — [/150]

STORY 4A — [/30]

STORY 4B — [/30]

SPELLING
5A — [/10]
5B — [/10]
5C — [/10]
SUB-TOTAL — [/30]

*Half this is your Spelling Score** — [/15]

HANDWRITING 6 — [/10]

WRITING TOTAL — [/85]

READING SCORE	National Curriculum Level	WRITING SCORE
150		85
145		
140		80
135		
130		75
125	LEVEL 6	
120		70
115		65
110		
105		60
100	LEVEL 5	
95		55
90		
85		50
80		45
75		
70		40
65	LEVEL 4	
60		35
55		
50		30
45		25
40		
35	LEVEL 3	20
30		
25		15
20		
15		10
10	LEVEL 2	
5		5
0	LEVEL 1	0

How to find your Level in English

You can work out which National Curriculum Level you have reached in English using the following method:

Work out your Reading Score by adding all your scores in Tests 1, 2 and 3. Mark the total with a cross in the Reading Score column on the left of the chart.

Work out your Writing Score by adding all your scores in Tests 4, 5 and 6. *Note your Spelling Scores must be halved before including in the total.* Mark the total with a cross in the Writing Score column on the left of the chart.

Draw a straight line from one cross to the other cross. The point at which your line crosses the centre line will show your National Curriculum Level for English. *See Level 3 example (arrow).*

WELL DONE!